Tom's ride

Story by Jenny Giles
Illustrations by Chantal Stewart

Dad said,

"Come on, Tom.

I will take you to the stores today."

"Oh, good," said Tom.

"May we go to the book store?"

"I can see some of your friends in the park," said Dad. "Let's go in."

"But I can't play on the slide and the swings like my friends," said Tom.

Tom's friends came running to see him.

"Come and look over here," said Jamie.

"A new tractor," said Tom. "I can play on **that**!"

Dad helped Tom up.

"I can see a word," said Tom.

"Read it to us," said Jamie.

"You are good at reading, Tom."

"Ch…" said Tom. "Chug!"

"This is **Chug the Tractor!**"

The children climbed on Chug.

"Take us for a ride, Tom," they said.

"Here we go," said Tom.
"We are going up the hill."

"**Up the hill**!" shouted his friends.

Tom laughed.

"Now we are going down the hill," he said.

"**Down the hill**!" shouted his friends.

Then all the children had to go home.

"We will come back and play on Chug again," said Jamie.

"Yes," said Tom.

"I had fun at the park today."